Greatest Ashes Moments

Written by Nick Hunter

Contents

Collins

Cricket's fiercest rivalry

For the cricketers of England and Australia, one contest is more important than any other. The winners of matches between these countries will lift one of the oldest and most famous trophies in sport – the Ashes.

England won the Ashes in 2015.

The two teams have been fierce **rivals** since the first English team toured Australia in 1861. The battle for the Ashes has raged over more than 300 matches. Australia and England's women cricketers have played each other since the 1930s. They now play for their own Ashes **trophy**.

The Ashes has created great sporting moments, heroes and villains. In this book, we'll ask which Ashes moments are the greatest of all.

Australian batsman Steve Smith celebrating an Ashes **century** in the 2015 series

3

The birth of the Ashes, 1882

The first great moment was actually a joke, which led to cricket's most famous trophy.

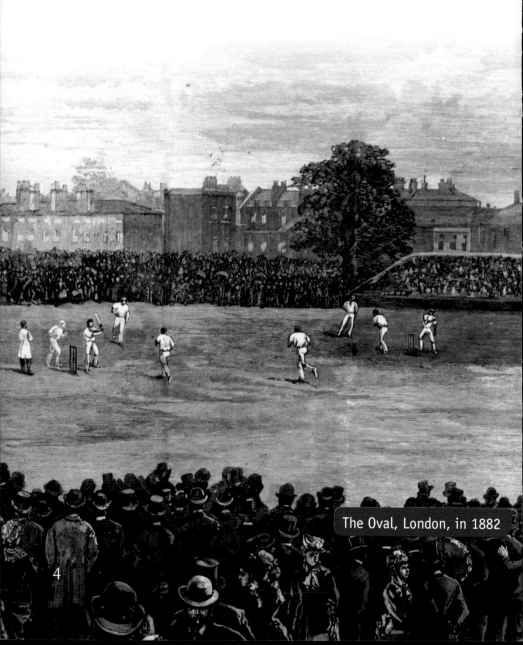

The Oval, London, in 1882

The Australian fast bowler, Fred "the Demon" Spofforth, terrified English batsmen. England's 11 players needed to score just 85 runs between them to win the **test match** at the Oval in 1882. Spofforth never gave up. He took 14 **wickets** in the match and England lost by eight runs.

Fred Spofforth

The ultimate ●●● test

The Ashes go to the winners of a series of test matches. In a test match, each side bats twice. The team that scores the most runs in their two **innings** is the winner. If the four innings are not completed after five days, the match is a draw.

The Oval test match was the first ever victory for Australia in England. *The Sporting Times* newspaper claimed that English cricket had "died at the Oval on 29th August, 1882". It joked that "the body will be **cremated** and the ashes taken to Australia".

WG Grace was England's most famous cricketer in 1882.

Twelve days later, England captain Ivo Bligh and his team set out on the two-month sea voyage to Australia. Bligh promised he'd "try to recover those ashes". During the tour, Bligh was given a small perfume bottle with some ashes inside. This is the trophy that England and Australia play for today.

The tiny Ashes urn

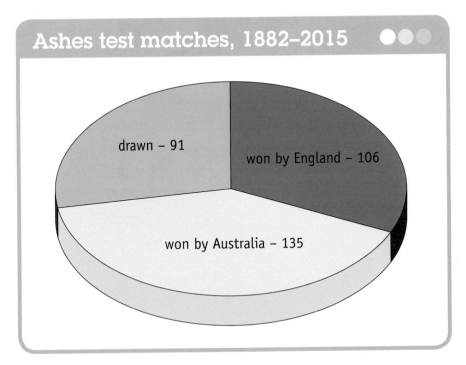

Ashes test matches, 1882–2015

drawn – 91

won by England – 106

won by Australia – 135

Bodyline, 1932–33

Sometimes the struggle to win the Ashes has caused real anger between players and fans. That's what happened in the Bodyline series of 1932–33.

England captain Douglas Jardine had to stop Australian batting genius Don Bradman if he wanted to win.

Douglas Jardine

Jardine hatched a plan. He asked lightning-fast bowler Harold Larwood to aim the ball at the batsmen's bodies. As they fended off the ball, it would fly into the waiting hands of a ring of **fielders** standing behind them.

bodyline bowling in action

England tried this "bodyline bowling" in the first test match at Sydney. Australia's players complained that the tactic was **unsporting**. The players didn't have the helmets and padding worn nowadays.

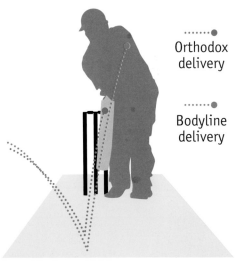

Orthodox delivery

Bodyline delivery

During the third test match in Adelaide, Bert Oldfield was hit on the head by Larwood's fearsome bowling. Australia's captain, Bill Woodfull, was furious. He said, "There are two teams out there. One is trying to play cricket and the other is not."

Harold Larwood ★★★

Larwood was one of the fastest bowlers ever. He refused to apologise for his bodyline bowling, saying he'd followed his captain's orders. He never played for England again.

England won the Ashes, but the Bodyline series led to angry letters between the English and Australian cricket authorities. The laws of cricket were changed to put an end to bodyline bowling.

The bodyline battle was front-page news.

Bradman's brilliance, 1937

Australia and England fans don't agree on much –
a triumph for one side is a tragedy for the other. But there
are no arguments about the greatest Ashes batsman of
all time. There has only ever been one Don Bradman.

Bradman scored 19
Ashes centuries in
37 test matches.
His highest score was
334 runs in 1930.

Many experts believe Bradman was at his best at Melbourne in 1937. Bradman was Australia's captain, and it wasn't going well. England were leading 2–0 in the series. People even questioned whether Bradman was the right man to lead Australia.

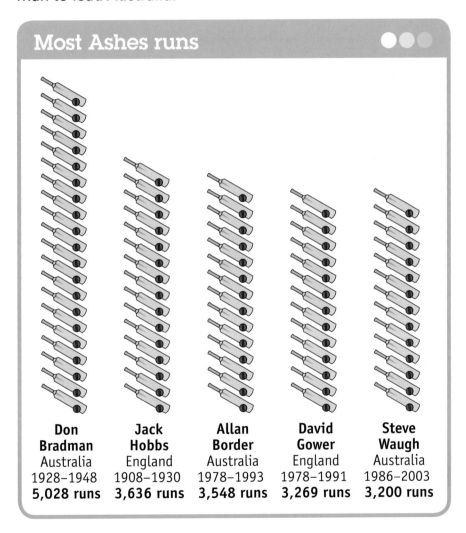

Most Ashes runs

Don Bradman	Jack Hobbs	Allan Border	David Gower	Steve Waugh
Australia	England	Australia	England	Australia
1928–1948	1908–1930	1978–1993	1978–1991	1986–2003
5,028 runs	**3,636 runs**	**3,548 runs**	**3,269 runs**	**3,200 runs**

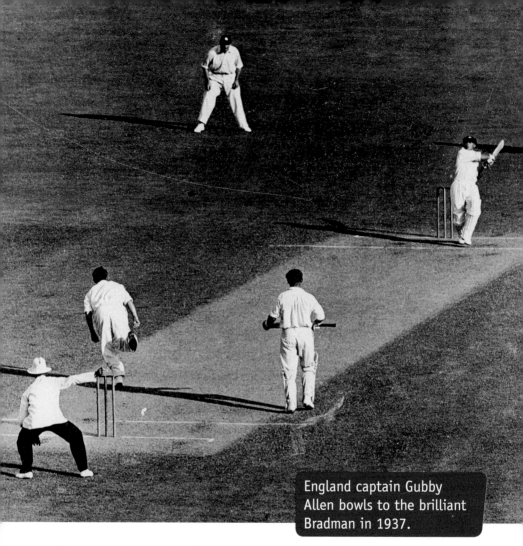

England captain Gubby Allen bowls to the brilliant Bradman in 1937.

Heavy rain meant that the ball was flying in all directions as it bounced off the sticky **pitch**. When Bradman came out to bat in Australia's second innings, only one batsman had scored more than 50 in the whole match. Bradman was battling illness as well as the English bowlers. He batted for nearly eight hours, scoring 270.

Australia won in Melbourne, watched by more than 350,000 people. They followed up with victories in the next two matches to claim the Ashes. Bradman scored centuries in both matches.

The Melbourne Cricket Ground is still the world's biggest.

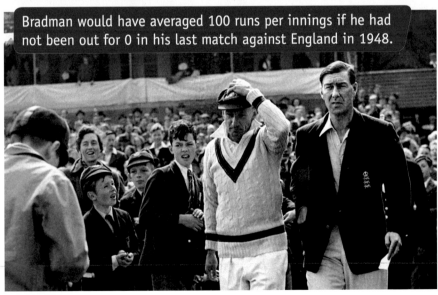

Bradman would have averaged 100 runs per innings if he had not been out for 0 in his last match against England in 1948.

Pitch perfect, 1956

The pitch can change a cricket match. Batsmen enjoy playing on pitches where the ball bounces evenly. Bowlers want the ball to **seam** or spin off the pitch.

Occasionally, the bowler's skill and the pitch combine to make batting almost impossible. Jim Laker's achievement at Manchester in 1956 will probably never be beaten.

Jim Laker

England scored 459 and Australia reached 48 before Laker took his first wicket with a sharply spinning ball. Fellow **spinner** Tony Lock took one wicket, but Laker took the other nine.

Heavy rain followed by sunshine made the pitch perfect for Laker's magic. He took all ten Australian wickets in the second innings. He finished the match with an astonishing 19 wickets for 90 runs.

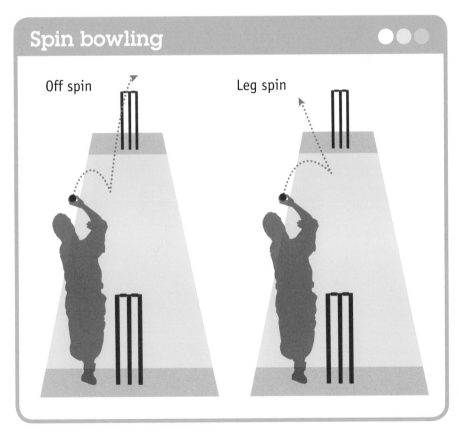

Spin bowling

Off spin

Leg spin

The impossible comeback, 1981

England's victory at Leeds in 1981 was not just about a team fighting back to win. Ian Botham and Bob Willis had hit rock bottom. Together they snatched victory from almost certain defeat.

Dennis Lillee was Australia's leading bowler.

Ian Botham ★ ★ ★

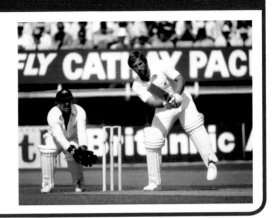

"Beefy" Botham was one of the greatest **all-rounders** to play in the Ashes. No England player has matched his 148 wickets against Australia. Botham also scored 1,673 runs, including four centuries.

England had lost the first match of the Ashes series. After a draw in the second test match, Ian Botham **resigned** as captain. Willis had been unwell and was almost left out of the team. The new captain was Mike Brearley.

Brearley knew how to inspire his star players.

England were 227 runs behind after both teams had batted once. In the second innings, England lost their seventh wicket for 135. It looked as if Australia would win without even having to bat again. But by then Botham was batting. His blistering 149 runs from just 148 balls left Australia needing 130 runs to win.

Botham's brilliance made him a hero to England's fans.

Now it was Willis's turn in the spotlight. The crowd roared the fast bowler on as he bowled. Willis took eight wickets as Australia were bowled out for 111. England had completed an amazing comeback.

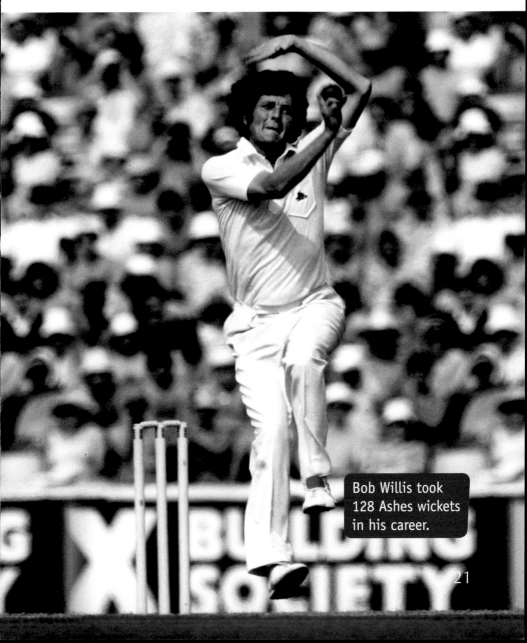

Bob Willis took 128 Ashes wickets in his career.

Ball of the century, 1993

Some great players burst on to the scene like cricketing superheroes. Shane Warne was an Australian Ashes hero from the first ball he bowled.

Shane Warne played in 36 Ashes tests.

The stout, bearded Mike Gatting wouldn't have been too worried about facing Shane Warne as he stepped up to bowl. The blond **leg spinner** looked like he'd come straight from the beach.

Gatting heard the spinning ball fizzing as it bounced outside his legs. It landed well away from the stumps. In an instant, the ball darted back sharply. Gatting looked behind him in horror. The ball had spun past his bat and pads before hitting the stumps.

Warne's unstoppable first ball was called the "Ball of the Century".

Gatting was stunned as he trudged off the field. So was everyone else who saw the ball, except perhaps Warne himself. Nothing had prepared the cricket world for his explosive impact on the Ashes.

In the years that followed, Warne took a total of 195 wickets – more than any other bowler in the history of the Ashes.

Warne helped to bowl Australia to victory in seven Ashes series.

Bowlers with most Ashes wickets ● ● ●

Shane Warne	Dennis Lillee	Glenn McGrath	Ian Botham
Australia	Australia	Australia	England
195	**167**	**157**	**148**

England's batsmen also had to withstand the fast, accurate bowling of Glenn McGrath during the 1990s and 2000s.

The greatest match, 2005

The 2005 Ashes was possibly the most exciting series of test cricket ever played. England hadn't won the Ashes for 18 years. Glenn McGrath bowled Australia to victory in the first test match. England fans feared they'd never win again.

Kevin Pietersen scored the most runs for England in 2005.

England were relieved when McGrath injured himself before the next match in Birmingham, and they scored 407 runs on the first day. As the match wore on, first one side and then the other seemed to be winning. Andrew Flintoff scored two 50s and took vital wickets. Shane Warne's bowling tormented the English.

Andrew "Freddie" Flintoff ★★★

Fiery all-rounder Flintoff was the star of the 2005 Ashes. He scored 402 runs and claimed 24 wickets.

Australia had to score 282 to win. At the end of the third day, they had 175, but England only needed to take two more wickets. The crowd expected an easy England win.

nervous fans hoping for an Ashes victory

What they got was
a nail-biting 99 minutes
of cricket. Australia's
batsmen edged closer to
the magic 282. With just three
more runs needed, the ball

That was close!

England's victory at
Birmingham in 2005 was
the closest test match in
Ashes history.

bounced off Michael Kasprowicz's glove and was caught by
the **wicketkeeper**. England won by two runs. Australia had
been beaten, but not without a fight.

Flintoff consoles Australian cricketer
Brett Lee after the closest finish ever.

Johnson's revenge, 2013–14

In July 2013, England won the Ashes 3–0 at home. They headed for Australia later that year to defend the trophy, full of confidence. But one Australian bowler was looking for revenge.

tough times for Mitchell Johnson

Mitchell Johnson had toured England in 2009. His fast **swing bowling** took wickets, but he struggled to bowl on target all the time. Things got worse as England's supporters jeered his mistakes from the stands. Johnson wasn't chosen for Australia's tour of England in 2013.

Michael Clarke

Australia's captain in 2013–14 was Michael Clarke. He played in Australia's 5–0 Ashes victory in 2006–07, but he also finished on the losing side in five Ashes series.

At Brisbane in November 2013, Johnson was back. Nearly every ball he bowled was on target. Some were aimed at the stumps; others bounced up towards the batsman's head. Johnson's nine wickets helped Australia to an easy win.

Johnson on form in 2013

Modern batters are protected by padding and helmets.

England's batsmen never recovered. They seemed to be terrified by the barrage of fast bowling from Johnson and his partner Ryan Harris. Australia won all five test matches, helped by 37 wickets from Johnson.

Whitewash ●●●

The Ashes series of 2013–14 was the third time that Australia had won all the matches in a five-match series. England have never managed this feat, called a whitewash.

60 all out, 2015

At the start of the 2015 series, most people expected Australia to win. There were several newer faces in the England team, such as all-rounders Ben Stokes and Moeen Ali. But after the third test, England were leading 2–1. Surely Australia would fight back.

Anyone with a ticket for the fourth test in Nottingham, needed to arrive on time. In Stuart Broad's first **over** of six balls, Chris Rogers and Steve Smith were out. Another Australian batsman was out in the next over.

seam

England bowler Stuart Broad made the shiny new cricket ball bounce off the seam and change direction.

Stuart Broad

In just over an hour, Australia had lost all ten wickets for just 60 runs. The England hero was Stuart Broad, who took eight wickets for just 15 runs.

Michael Clarke leads his team off the field after a disastrous day in Nottingham.

In a test match, both sides have two chances to bat. If England batted badly, Australia might still have had a chance. By the end of the day, England were more than 200 runs ahead. They won the match in just three days, and reclaimed the Ashes.

England's Joe Root scored a brilliant century after Australia's collapse.

Shortest innings ●●●

Australia's score of 60 all out wasn't the lowest in Ashes history. But their innings lasted just 111 balls, making it the shortest Ashes innings since 1936.

England captain Alastair Cook with the Ashes trophy.

From Magic Myrtle to Perfect Perry

England and Australia's women cricketers first played each other in Brisbane, Australia, in 1934. England all-rounder Myrtle Maclagan dominated the first test matches. She took seven wickets for just ten runs at Brisbane and followed up by scoring a century in the next match in Sydney.

The two teams have played for the Women's Ashes trophy since 1998. The contest is now played over one test match as well as one day and **Twenty20** games. Each side bats once in these games.

The Women's Ashes trophy contains the ashes of a cricket bat.

Charlotte Edwards

England's batting star Charlotte Edwards has scored more than 1,500 runs in the Ashes. She was captain when England won the trophy in 2013 and 2014.

Ellyse Perry of Australia was named player of the series in both 2013–14 and 2015. Perry's greatest bowling performance came in the test match at Canterbury. Perry destroyed England's batting, taking six wickets for 32 runs in the second innings.

The brilliant all-rounder finished the series with the most runs and wickets to her name, as her team claimed the Ashes in 2015.

Australia's winning team in 2015

Ellyse Perry

Perry was still only 24 when she dominated the Ashes in 2015. Her all-round skills aren't limited to cricket. Perry has played soccer for Australia in the Women's World Cup.

What's the greatest?

A great Ashes moment can be many different things.
Cricket is a team game, but we often remember
the performances of brilliant players such as
Don Bradman, Shane Warne or Stuart Broad.

Even the greatest bowlers
need fielders to catch the ball.

Players' skills are built by years of practice. But many of the greatest Ashes moments also show qualities such as teamwork, sportsmanship and leadership. Great sportspeople keep battling even when it seems the game is lost.

Every cricket fan has his or her own favourite moment. Your greatest Ashes moment could still be in the future.

Respecting the other team is always important.

Glossary

all-rounders players who are skilled at both batting and bowling

century score of 100 or more by a batter

cremated burnt

fielders players on the team that's not batting who stand on the cricket field to stop or catch the ball when it's hit

innings turn at batting of a team or individual batter. In a test match, each team gets two turns to bat or innings.

leg spinner a bowler who bowls right-arm with a wrist spin action

over when a bowler bowls six times in a row. After each over, another player bowls an over from the other end of the pitch.

pitch the area of grass, 20 metres long, on which the ball is bowled to the batsman

resigned stepped down or stopped doing something, such as leaving a job

rivals people or things that are aiming to be more successful in achieving something

seam stitching around the middle of a cricket ball. The ball can change direction if it bounces on the seam.

spinner bowler who makes the ball spin

swing bowling bowling that makes the ball change direction slightly as it moves through the air

Twenty20 a short, fast-paced type of cricket, often called T20

test match cricket match in which two national sides have two innings each, played over several days

trophy prize or cup for winning a contest

unsporting unfair or against the agreed rules of a game

wickets either the three stumps and bails that a batter stands in front of in cricket, or the word used for when a batter is out

wicketkeeper fielder who stands behind the stumps when the ball is bowled to catch the ball

Index

Ashes timeline

 Years when England held the ashes

Years when Australia held the ashes

1882
The Ashes are born after Australia's first win in England.

1932–33
Bodyline series led by England captain Douglas Jardine and Australia's Bill Woodfull

1930
Don Bradman scores 334 – the highest individual score for Australia.

1934
First women's test match between England and Australia takes place in Brisbane.

1937
Bradman scores 270 in Melbourne test match.

1956
Jim Laker takes 19 wickets in test match at Manchester.

2013–14
Australia win Ashes series 5-0 helped by 37 wickets from Mitchell Johnson.

2005
England win closest ever Ashes match by just two runs at Birmingham.

1993
Shane Warne's first ball in Ashes test matches bowls Mike Gatting.

1981
Ian Botham scores 149 not out and Bob Willis takes 8 wickets for 43 to win Leeds test match.

1998
Ashes trophy introduced for women's test matches.

2015
Ellyse Perry stars in Australia victory in Women's Ashes.

2015
Stuart Broad takes 8 wickets for 15 as Australia all out for 60 at Nottingham.

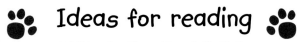

Ideas for reading

Written by Clare Dowdall, PhD
Lecturer and Primary Literacy Consultant

Reading objectives:
- retrieve and record information from non-fiction
- discuss a wide range of non-fiction texts and reference books
- read books that are structured in different ways
- draw inferences and justify these with evidence

Spoken language objectives:
- participate in discussions, presentations, performances, role play, improvisations and debates

Curriculum links: Physical Education: competitive games

Resources: ICT; equipment for playing a cricket-style game, paper and pencils, ICT and sports books for research.

Build a context for reading
- Ask children to share what they know about the game of cricket and what is fun about it.
- Read the book's title and look at the front cover. Ask children to share any knowledge that they have about the Ashes.
- Read the blurb together. Establish that the Ashes is the name of a long-standing cricket competition between Australia and England.

Understand and apply reading strategies
- Turn to the contents. Ask children to read through them and notice how the book is organised and what sort of information book this is (a recount in chronological order).
- Ask children to read pp2–7 independently to find out what "The Ashes" actually are. Challenge children to recount what they have read orally. Ask questions and prompt for detail.
- Focus on page 6. Check that children understand the "joke" in the sports paper and the use of metaphorical language *the body will be cremated and the ashes taken to Australia*. Explain that *the body* refers to the game of cricket, if necessary.